D1442224

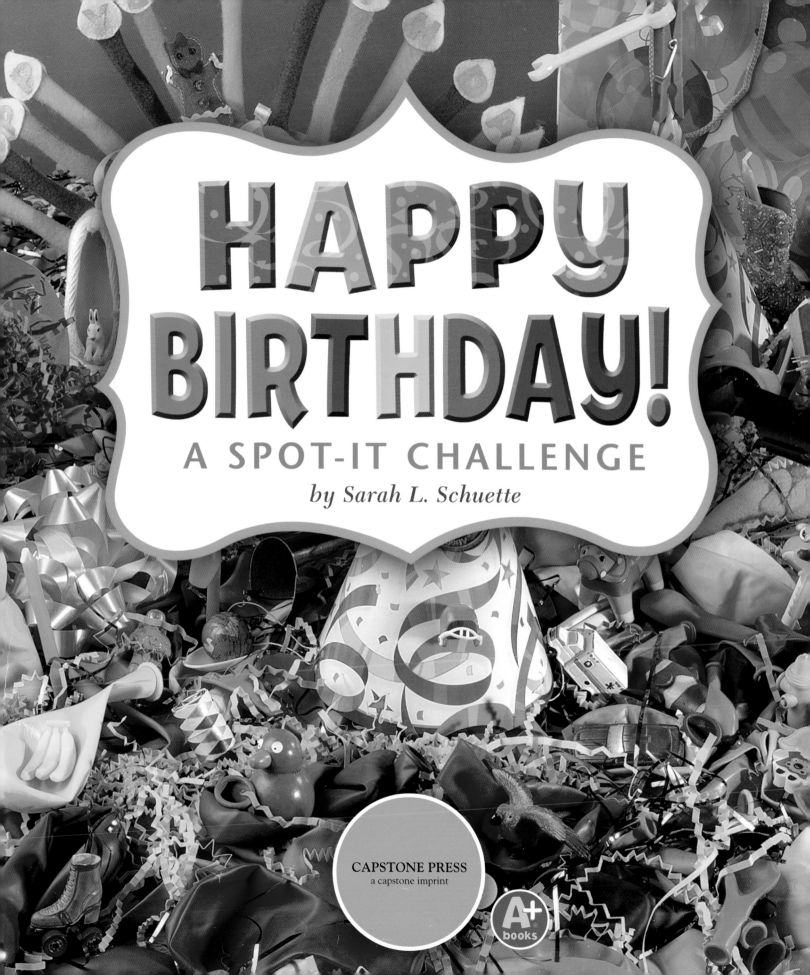

HAPPY BIRTHDAY!

A SPOT-IT CHALLENGE

by Sarah L. Schuette

CAPSTONE PRESS
a capstone imprint

A+
books

A+ Books are published by Capstone Press,
1710 Roe Crest Drive, North Mankato, Minnesota 56003.
www.capstonepub.com

Books published by Capstone Press are manufactured with paper
containing at least 10 percent post-consumer waste.

Library of Congress Cataloging-in-Publication Data
Schuette, Sarah, L., 1976–
Happy Birthday: A Spot-It Challenge / by Sarah L. Schuette
p. cm (A+ Books. Spot it.)
Summary: "Simple Text invites the reader to find items hidden in birthday-themed
photographs"—Provided by publisher.
ISBN 978-1-4296-7560-4 (library binding)
1. Picture puzzles—juvenile literature. I. Title. II. Series.
GV1507.P47 S377 2012
793.73—dc22   2011041602

Credits
Shelly Lyons, editor; Ted Williams, designer; Laura Manthe, production specialist;
    Sarah Schuette, photo stylist; Marcy Morin, photo scheduler; Eliza Cate Lynard, photo assistant

Photo Credits
All photos by Capstone Studio: Karon Dubke, except: Shutterstock: Jennifer Johnson, BlueCherry
    Graphics, title texture

Capstone would like to thank Pet Expo for the use of a live rabbit for page 22
of this book.

The author dedicates this book to her cousin Morgan Schmidt.

Note to Parents, Teachers, and Librarians
Spot It is an interactive series that supports literacy development and reading enjoyment.
Readers utilize visual discrimination skills to find objects among fun-to-peruse photographs
with busy backgrounds. Readers also build vocabulary through thematic groupings, develop
visual memory ability through repeated readings, and improve strategic and associative
thinking skills by experimenting with different visual search methods.

Printed in the United States of America in North Mankato, Minnesota.
102011   006405CGS12

Table of Contents

Invited

Can you spot ...

- a squirrel?
- a dove?
- a camel?
- a dragon?
- a lamp?
- a camera?

Wrap It Up

Can you spot ...

- a helicopter?
- a purple star?
- a tiger?
- a rock?
- a key?
- a lizard?

Let's Play

Can you spot …
- a baseball?
- a shamrock?
- an apple?
- a panda?
- a birdhouse?
- a globe?

9

Let's Eat Cake!

Can you spot …

- a rabbit?
- two presents?
- a mouse?
- a spray bottle?
- a ruler?
- a purse?

Strike

Can you spot …
- a padlock?
- a pair of wax lips?
- a football?
- a leopard?
- a clock?
- a cupcake?

Fiesta!

Can you spot …

- a spider web?
- a scarecrow?
- a snail?
- a guitar?
- a maple leaf?
- a boot?

Slumber Party

Can you spot …

- an igloo?
- a question mark?
- a yo-yo?
- a pair of jeans?
- a fork?
- a monarch butterfly?

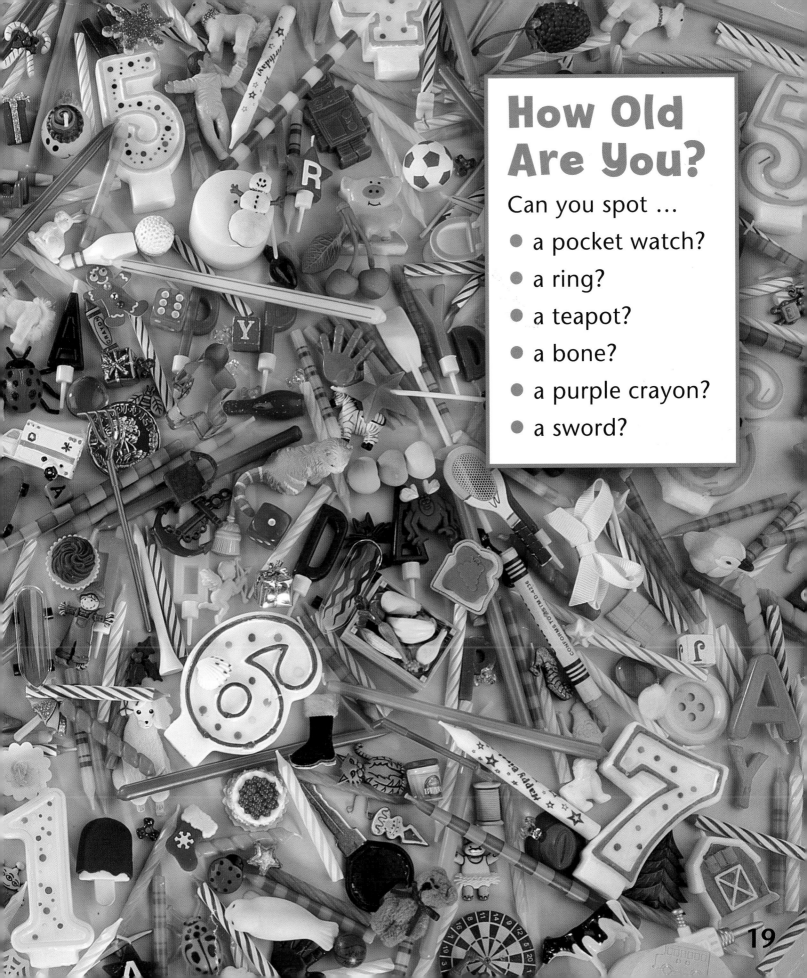

How Old Are You?

Can you spot …

- a pocket watch?
- a ring?
- a teapot?
- a bone?
- a purple crayon?
- a sword?

Hats Off!

Can you spot …
- a pony?
- a spoon?
- a carrot?
- an ambulance?
- a soccer ball?
- an alien?

Tricky

Can you spot ...
- a turkey?
- a parrot?
- a shell?
- a pineapple?
- a jeep?
- a fire truck?

23

Gifts for Me?

Can you spot …

- a cactus?
- a playing card?
- a watch?
- a raspberry?
- an ice skate?
- a cockroach?

Pirate Party

Can you spot ...

- a seal?
- a rooster?
- a lantern?
- a bobber?
- a tennis ball?
- a ghost?

Spot Even More!

Invited

Try to spot a fire truck, three little pigs, two owls, a hot air balloon, and two U.S. flags.

Wrap It Up

This time find a toucan, two pumpkins, two babies, and a bee.

Let's Play

Now look for a schoolhouse, the number 10, a chili pepper, two milk cartons, and a sea horse.

Let's Eat Cake!

Take another look to find a bunch of bananas, a honey bee, a princess dress, and a pine tree.

Strike

Time to find two bats, a golf ball, a raccoon, and a spinning top.

Fiesta!

Now spot a jackhammer, a Christmas tree, a robot, and two hair brushes.

Slumber Party

See if you can find a dog food bowl, a tomato slice, a corncob, a policeman, and a slice of pizza.

How Old Are You?

Check for a hat, a palm tree, a fortune cookie, a baseball bat, and two boat oars.

Hats Off!

See if you can spot a wrench, two clothespins, a ninja, a car, and a crown.

Tricky

Try to find a box of cereal, a whistle, the letter "Z", a circular saw, and two snowflakes.

Gifts for Me?

Try to find a spider, a toaster, a pineapple, and a pack of gum.

Pirate Party

See if you can spot a pickle, an octopus, a goldfish, a unicorn, and some French fries.

Extreme Spot-It Challenge

Just can't get enough Spot-It action?
Here's an extra challenge. Try to spot:

- a starfish
- two shovels
- a fire hydrant
- a sheep
- a dragonfly
- a cow
- a bow
- a rat
- a mermaid
- a hammer
- a blue bird
- a cobweb
- a pig
- a pair of binoculars
- a piano
- a golf tee
- two flies

Read More

Chedru, Delphine. *Spot It Again!: Find More Hidden Creatures.* New York: Abrams Books for Young Readers, 2011.

Marks, Jennifer L. *Fun and Games: A Spot-It Challenge.* Spot It. Mankato, Minn.: Capstone Press, 2009.

Schuette, Sarah L. *Animal Fun: A Spot-It Challenge.* Spot It. Mankato, Minn.: Capstone Press, 2012.

Internet Sites

FactHound offers a safe, fun way to find Internet sites related to this book. All of the sites on FactHound have been researched by our staff.

Here's all you do:

Visit *www.facthound.com*

Type in this code: **9781429675604**

Check out projects, games and lots more at
www.capstonekids.com